STRENGTH
IN WAITING

ROBBIN STASNY

ISBN 978-1-64028-169-1 (Paperback)
ISBN 978-1-64028-170-7 (Digital)

Christian Faith Publishing, Inc.
296 Chestnut Street
Meadville, PA 16335
www.christianfaithpublishing.com

Printed in the United States of America

PREFACE

Strength in Waiting was written to help others learn how to deal with crisis in their lives. As most of you are aware, these life trials are very real and sometimes can knock us off our feet at times. The only way I have found to handle what life throws at me is to have a personal relationship with God and his son Jesus Christ. My favorite family verse from the Bible is Philippians 4:13, "I can do all things through Christ who strengthens me." To me, this verse means that no matter what comes my way, I can deal with it as long as God is right there beside me. I know he will never give me more than I can handle.

The book of Isaiah speaks about promises of restoration and redemption. I particularly like Isaiah 40:31 and 64:4. These two verses tell us that when we wait on the Lord, he will renew our strength. When we wait on the Lord, he will do things in our lives we can't possibly imagine. Our God is an awesome God and through a personal relationship with him, we can weather any storm. Waiting on the Lord is so important that even King David wrote about in his Psalms. (Psalms 27:14). In fact, David believed it to be the key to a victorious life. Think about it folks, just hold on a little bit longer, seek God and his strength to get you through these trials you are facing this very moment.

In the book of Micah, Micah believed the importance of an ongoing relationship with God and Jesus Christ. He also believed that God would hear him when he prayed. Interesting enough, the word "wait" means to tarry, trust, expect, and be patient. This word is often translated as "hope". We are to patiently hope and wait upon the Lord for he will answer us.

Micah 7:7, "Therefore I will look to the Lord, I will wait for the God of my salvation, My God will hear me."

STRENGTH IN WAITING

"I can do all things through Christ who strengthens me"
(Philippians 4:13).

DIRECTIONS FOR LIFE

I will instruct you and teach you
In the way you should go;
I will counsel you with
With my eye upon you.
Psalm 32:8

Wouldn't it be awesome if life came with some sort of guide to instruct us on how to handle everything that gets thrown at us? If we had this guide, we would all know which path to choose and perhaps never make a mistake or miss an opportunity. Well guess what, there is a guide for all of life's situations. It is called the Bible. In fact, there are approximately 54 verses in the Bible that discuss "direction".

The Bible is written words from God on how to live our life. The Bible is written words on how to handle difficult situations, questionable situations, our life's purpose, and so much more. It is written instruction on what God wants us to do. The Bible reveals to us what we should believe about God and what God requires of us, his children. Everything we need to know is in this book.

Start each day with the words of God. Psalm 5:1–12, especially verse 8, "Lead me, O Lord, in your righteousness because of my enemies; make you way straight before my face." Psalm 5 is a great Psalm when you need guidance. As in all journey's, it is always a good idea to get directions before you start your journey. If you get directions before, you will not get lost.

In requesting God's directions for our lives, we must not forget about his son, Jesus, and all the steps he took specifically for us. In addition, we need to learn to trust God in directing our steps. Sometimes this seems slow, one step at a time. Our God loves us so much and wants to direct our steps in life. Remember the journey may not always be smooth. Abraham had to leave his native country as God directed him to another location to spread his word. Although Abraham was scared, he trusted God enough to do as he was instructed, wherever that might be. If we do as God directs, he will bless us as we follow in the steps he directs.

If we stay in God's word and listen to the Holy Spirit, we can learn so much about what plans God has for us. We can discover great and marvelous things only God can provide. In 1 Peter 1:22–23, "Since you have purified your souls in obeying the truth through the Spirit in sincere love of the brethren, love one another fervently with a pure heart, having been born again, not of corruptible seed but incorruptible, through the word of God, which lives and abides forever." We will still make mistakes because we are human and sometimes wonder from the path we are on; however, if we keep focused and stay in the Word, we can make amends to those mistakes.

Did you know that God does not allow any person or thing to keep you from your destiny? Destiny is God's purpose for your life. You are ordained or appointed future according to God's divine will. Samson's destiny was known before he was born, yet he missed it due to poor choices. Saul and Solomon also made poor choices which took them away from their destiny. Thanks to Jesus Christ dying on the cross, our poor choices cannot take us from our destiny. The Old Testament tells us we each have our own individual destiny.

Ephesians 1:7–10,

"7 In Him we have redemption through His blood, the forgiveness of sins, according to the riches of His grace

8 which He made to abound toward us in all wisdom and prudence,

9 having made known to us the mystery of His will, according to His good pleasure, which he purposed in Himself,

10 that in the dispensation of the fullness of the times He might gather together in one all things in Christ, both which are in heaven and which are on earth—in Him.

The obstacles you may be facing this very day may seem bigger, stronger, and more powerful than you can handle, but our God is big enough, he can handle them. Do you have a problem that has not gone away? Does it seem as if God has put you on the back burner? Is your marriage experiencing difficulty? Does your son or daughter have a drug problem? The list of our trials could be these or other things that are not listed. What is on your list does not matter. What does matter is the fact that you believe God is bigger.

Our God is bigger!

He knows how to make things right and when to make things right.

Genesis 37:41—is the story of Joseph—all the right things came in to place in order for Joseph to become all that God had planned him to be. God used all the setbacks and crisis in Joseph's life to mold and shape him into the man of God he eventually became.

God uses all these setbacks in your life to move you forward. I know it doesn't make sense, but don't lose faith and most of all, do not give up (Genesis 45:1–28). God is still in control of your situation, and he is working all things out for good. There are numerous stories in the Bible where God has used hardships in people's lives to mold and shape them into the person he created them to be. Think of a piece of steel becoming a useful item. There has to be work done on it. The steel has to be refined. This takes a certain process and a certain amount time.

Just because you cannot see what's going on does not mean that God is not working behind the scenes. He has not forgotten you, even if you forget about God. Even if you stray so far off the path that you think you can never find your way back, God never leaves us. We are always allowed to make our own decisions, and sometimes those decisions cause us difficult trials. No matter, God is still behind the scenes. And in fact, you may be surprised by all that is happening behind the scenes to fix the problems you are facing this very day.

In my personal experience, when things are going all wrong, and it seems that God is not paying attention, a song will come on the Christian radio station or a dear friend will text me a Bible verse that exactly pertains to what I am going through. This song or verse is exactly what I needed at that exact moment. Coincidence? No, it was God reminding me that he is still working on the situation and to trust him to complete it. He never leaves us alone. He constantly reminds us he is there with us during the difficulties. You just have to look for him. He never leaves us alone. He constantly reminds us he is there with us during this time. Whether the situation is work, friends, or family; it makes no difference. God always lets me know that he is still in control and to trust him even when I am having doubts, even when I cannot physically see anything changing or taking place regarding that difficult situation.

Remember God works from the inside first, so there may not appear to be any changes, but I am confident that my God is working and will finish what he began.

Did you know that you are always on God's mind? Always. God's plan of salvation was devised before the world was ever created. His plan of salvation was devised before you were born. He was thinking of you in 750 BC. He was thinking of you when he promised that he would rescue all people from their sins. You were in that rescue.

Psalm 39 tells us of God's perfect knowledge of man.

"O Lord, You have searched me and known me,
You know my sitting down and my rising up;
You understand my thought afar off.
You comprehend my path and my lying down,
And are acquainted with all my ways.
For there is not a word on my tongue,
But behold, O Lord, You know it altogether.
You have hedged me behind and before,
And laid your hand upon me.
Such knowledge is too wonderful for me;
It is high, I cannot attain it.
Where can I go from Your Spirit?
Or where can I flee from Your presence?
If I ascend into heaven, You are there;
If I make my bed in hell, behold, You are there.
I take the wings of the morning,
And dwell in the uttermost parts of the sea.

Even there Your hand shall lead me,
And your right hand shall hold me.
If I say, Surely the darkness shall not hide from you,
But the night shines as the day;
The darkness and the light are both alike to you,
For you formed my inward parts;
You covered me in my mother's womb.
I will praise you, for I am fearfully and wonderfully made;
Marvelous are Your works,
And that my soul knows very well.
My frame was not hidden from You,
When I was made in secret,
And skillfully wrought in the lowest parts of the earth.
Your eyes saw my substance, not being yet unformed.
And in your book they all were written.
The days fashioned for me,
When as yet there were none of them.
How precious also are your thoughts to me, O god!
How great is the sum of them!
If I should count them, they would be
more in number than the sand;
When I awake, I am still with You.
Oh, that You would slay the wicked, O God!
Depart from me, therefore you bloodthirsty men.
For they speak against You wickedly;
Your enemies take Your name in vain.
Do I not hate them, O Lord, who hate you?
And do I not loathe those who rise up against you?
I hate them with perfect hatred;
I count them my enemies.
Search me, O God, and know my heart;
Try me, and know my anxieties;

And see if there is an wicked way in me,
And lead me in the way everlasting."
(NSFLB)

How often do you think about God? Do you only think of him to complain? Do you ever just meditate on his love, faithfulness, power, and devotion? When was the last time you praised him just because he is your God? Do you just seek him when there are difficulties? Psalm 139 tells us that God's thoughts about you outnumber the grains of the sand. Have you ever been to the beach and looked at all the sand area—it's massive and uncountable. Wow! I once read a note as if it were from God, "Sit quietly in my presence while I bless you. Make your mind like a still pool of water, ready to receive whatever thoughts I drop into it. Rest in my sufficiency as you consider the challenges this day presents. Do not wear yourself out by worrying about whether you can cope with the pressures. Keep looking to me and communicating with me as we walk through this day together. Take time to rest by the wayside for I am not in a hurry. A leisurely pace accomplishes more than hurried striving. When you rush, you forget who you are and more importantly *whose you are*. Remember that you are royalty in my kingdom." That says it all really. If we were to sit quietly and rest in God's presence, what a difference it would make in our lives, our daily activities, everything really. Let's break some of this down to understand it more clearly.

"If you sit quietly and just be, you will experience a great peace which nothing can surpass." Perhaps, God is saying this, "If you sit quietly and just be, you will experience a great peace only I can give you."

"Make your mind like a still pool of water, ready to receive whatever thoughts I drop into it." Perhaps God is asking that you let him take over our mind and he will leave you little bits of encouragement. He will leave you messages to get you through this difficult time."

"Rest in my sufficiency, as you consider the challenges this day presents." Here, God is saying for us to start our day with him, this will allow him to be with us when we face challenges of the day.

"Do not wear yourself out by worrying about whether you can cope with the pressures. Keep looking to me and communicating with me as we walk through this day together." God is simply reminding us that when we put our focus on him during the trials, we become stronger.

"Take time to rest by the wayside, for I am not in a hurry." To rest is healing to the human body, so why not rest in God during the trials of life. Give it all to him and experience a complete rest of mind, body, and soul.

Interesting enough before God sent His son Jesus to come to Earth and die on the cross, he thought of you and I. In God's book, the Bible, we can learn all of this. He knew everything about you, all the things you would do, all the times you would get off the path and yet he still sent Jesus to save you, to save us all from ourselves. He loved you and I that much!

God loves us this much!! I used to tell my children this and hold out my arms straight. Then they would do it back. How much more does God love us? He loved us so much that he sent his son to die on the cross.

In the Old Testament, there are specific steps and actions to take in order to become purified so that one would be able to partake in the ceremonial worship at the tabernacle. Not everyone was able to participate in the ceremonial worship. Only a select few were ever able to do this.

To be purified, you had to be made ceremonial clean, a ritual bath to purify the soul and remove contaminants. To be ritually pure means to be free of some flaw or uncleanliness so there could be contact with holy objects, especially the holy presence of God in worship. In Numbers 8:5–12, there is a reference to this process.

5 "Then the Lord spoke to Moses, saying:

6 "Take the Levites and cleanse them *ceremonially.*

7 Thus you shall do to them to cleanse them; Sprinkle water of purification on them, and let them shave all their body, and let them wash their clothes, and so make themselves clean.

8 Then let them take a young bull with its gain offering of fine flour mixed with oil, and you shall take another young bull as a sin offering.

9 And you shall bring the Levites before the tabernacle of meeting, and you shall gather together the whole congregation of the children of Israel.

10 So you shall bring the Levites before the Lord, and the children of Israel shall lay their hands on the Levites;

11 and Aaron shall offer the Levites before the Lord, like a wave offering from the children of Israel, that they may perform the work of the Lord.

12 Then the Levites shall lay their hands on the heads of the young bulls, and you shall offer one as a sin offering; and the other as a burnt offering to the Lord, to make atonement for the Levites."

If one was purified, then they could participate in worship. Purification was intended for body and soul. Let me say that again, PURIFICATION was intended for BODY AND SOUL. This purification ritual, sometimes took days to accomplish. It was a necessary process and it was required; before anyone could partake in the ceremonial worship. Very few people were allowed to do this.

In Psalms 24:4, "He who has clean hands and a pure heart." These specific steps in the purification process had a final step, that step being sacrifice (this was usually a lamb). Because of the cross, Jesus became the final step. He became the ultimate sacrifice. He died to bring total purification—no more steps are needed. No more days of preparation. It was done! Anyone can come and worship God. Anyone! Not just a select few.

I guess you could say Jesus is life! He is "our" life. Without him, we are lost. Without him, we are not complete. Have you made him your Lord and Savior?

Through his blood, we became cleansed. By his blood, we are forgiven.

We get to start fresh every day, isn't that totally awesome?

Jesus did all of this for you and me. 1 John 1:7–9, "But if we walk in the light as He is in the light, we have fellowship with one another, and the blood of Jesus Christ His son cleanses us from all sin. If we say that we have no sin, we deceive ourselves, and the truth is not in us. If we confess our sins, He is faithful and just to forgive us our sins and to cleanse us from all unrighteousness." No matter what we have done, we can be cleansed from our unrighteousness.

Did you realize that when we walk in the light, it is a test of fellowship with God? The life of fellowship is a life that is continually cleansed from sin by the blood of Jesus because we are human and sin. His sacrifice on the cross allows this. This life of fellowship also includes our relationships with one another. A walk in the light is living accountable before God and before man. Have you ever heard the old saying, "Don't just talk the talk, but walk the walk?" Professional football player, Tim Tebow portrays this saying in his daily life. It has not made it easy for him to get work in the NFL because of his continued outward display of his Christian beliefs and actions on the field and in the locker room. He now plays for the minor league baseball team once, when a person in the bleechers was sick, he went over and prayed for that person until the ambulance arrived. It was automatic action for him to do this and he doesn't even think twice about it. It is part of his "nature." If we are to be an example of Christ to those around us, then we must be aware of our actions and have accountability for those actions. The only way we can do this is by allowing the Holy Spirit to guide our actions to be able to walk the path we were born to proceed on. This is not always easy and we will get side tracked, that's just part of life. If we follow the Holy Spirit, he will help the seeds God planted in us grow to fruition. I remind you that this does not and will not happen overnight.

I know most of you realize that from the time we pray and ask God to help us in a certain situation, sometimes, we discover that there is a waiting period before we see any change. This waiting period can be one hour, one day, one year, and so on. I think we should keep in mind that God's time is not like our time, so everyone's circumstances will be different. The point is that during this waiting period, we sometimes get impatient. We seem to have a set plan of how the situation should workout, and if God does not answer us as we imagined, we get upset and sometimes turn away from God. We keep asking for the same thing because we are not getting the results we want or results at all. I want to let you know that God does hear us the first time. There can be any number of reasons that he has not responded to our prayers. Perhaps, we should be patient during the waiting period and see the Glory of God take place.

Sometimes, circumstances seem to take months before you will see God bring something to completion. It is not easy to keep the faith even though I know from past history with God; he is faithful and will do what he promised he will do. His ways have always been best. We get discouraged when we do not see immediate results because of this microwave world we live in. God does not work that way. He is working the situation out in his time and his time is always perfect. This is where our faith must come in and sustain us until we are through the storm. When we face a long delay in our situation becoming resolved, doubt begins to creep in and cause us to have weak faith. The devil loves to creep in and make us lack faith in God, to worry and fret over things most of the time we have no control over.

Jeremiah 29:11 tells us, "For I know the plans I have for you, declares the Lord. Plans to prosper you and not to harm you, plans to give you hope and a future." These are not just words people? God does what he says he will do. Trust him today, let him take the reins, and be in control so you can be a peace. There is nothing like the peace of God, which surpasses all understanding. Worrying gets you nowhere anyway. In fact, stress makes you believe that everything has to happen immediately while faith assures you that everything will happen in God's timing. Psalm 33:11, "But the plans of the Lord stand time forever, the purpose of his heart through all generations." (NIV). I can assure you God's plans are perfect for your situation. Keep the faith and wait patiently.

In Jeremiah 33:3, God tells us, "Call to me and I will answer you, and show you great and mighty things, which you do not know."

John 16:24 also tells us, "Until now you have asked nothing in My name. Ask and you will receive, that your joy may be full."

1 John 5:14–15, "Now this is the confidence that we have in Him, that if we ask anything according to His will, He hears us. And if we know that he hears us, whatever we ask, we know that we have the petitions that we have asked of Him."

Matthew 7:7, "Ask, and it will be given to you; seek, and you will find; knock, and it will be opened to you."

All of these verses were written to confirm to us that God does hear us when we pray. He also answers us when we pray. The answer just may take a little longer than we anticipate. He sometimes needs to work things out behind the scenes before the situation gets resolved. I once read that the wait during these trials is more about "experiencing God" than the delay itself. Sometimes, the answers are not as we expected as well.

James 1:6–8, "But when you ask, you must believe and not doubt, because the one who doubts is like a wave of the sea, blown and tossed by the wind. That person should not expect to receive anything from the Lord. Such a person is double-minded and unstable in all they do."

God always keeps his word and he never breaks any promises that he makes with you. This does not mean that he will answer you immediately. Sometimes, I believe that during this waiting period, God is trying to build up our character. Sometimes, he is trying to teach you and I patience. All things are for God's glory, not ours. It is never about us, people! So if you are waiting on an answer from God on something you have prayed about, perhaps you are not ready to receive it yet. Perhaps God needs to do some work inside you to get your ready for his glory.

Psalm 40:5, "Many, Lord my God, are the wonders you have done, the things you planned for us. None can compare with you; were I to speak and tell of your deeds, they would be too many to declare."

Perhaps the person you have been praying about needs some work done in them and God is doing this very thing. Just because you cannot see anything happening does not mean that he is not doing work. God works from the inside, and sometimes this inside work takes time.

The Bible is filled with numerous examples of how powerful our God is. He is bigger than any crisis you are facing. He can part the waters of the Red Sea; he can send manna from heaven daily to feed his people.

So I guess a good question to ask yourself is this, "Is your praise and prayer time with God performed as part of a regular routine procedure or is it only when there is a crisis, a storm or difficulties, or is it only when you can find the time in your busy schedule? I realize we all have busy lies with work, family, etc. But God needs to be first. No more roller coaster become steadfast and strong. Why not start today.

Here is something to consider while waiting in your storm. There are many great people in the Bible who had to wait as well. Abraham and his wife Sarah had to wait almost 100 years for the child God promised they would have. Noah, remember him and the ark, he had to wait 120 years for the flood. During that time, he was made fun of. Guess what, Jesus, the son of God, waited thirty years before he began his public ministry. All of these examples prove God is with us and he will do what he says he will do.

Heavenly Father, thank you for your continued wisdom and guidance in my life. As I share with you y requests for this day, I ask for your wisdom and protection to surround me and give me direction for all the steps I will take from this day forward according to your will.

In Jesus' name I pray these things,
Amen

NO MORE ROLLER COASTER

The steps of a man are established by the Lord,
When he delights in his ways, though he fall,
He shall not be cast headlong,
For the Lord upholds his hand.
Psalm 37:23–24

When you were a child and just learning about prayer, you only turned to God when there was a crisis, instead of having a regular daily routine with him. In order to grow in Christ, we must have a daily routine first thing before we start our day. In order to grow in Christ, we must have a daily routine first thing before we start our day. Why not step off that roller coaster ride and get on a routine of regular praise and prayer time with our faithful God. There was never a promise of perfect life and no storms or problems. Just a promise that God would be with us during the storms of life, sometimes if necessary, to carry us. He does have to carry us when the burden gets too great. Allow him to do what he needs to do.

If we become so in tune with God's word and God himself that when a storm comes our way, we remain calm, then we have grown up. Our faith is steadfast and it is at this moment that we can feel a sense of peace because "our routine process" has kicked in. This is something we should all aim for in our walk with Christ. It will take some practice.

I can tell you that this does not happen overnight. This so-called routine reaction comes from daily practice just like anything in life. In order to be good, we have to practice. Someone once told me that it is a choice to be happy when things are going all wrong.

Did you hear that? It is a choice to be happy in the midst of trials, sorrows, and disappointments.

Jesus is life! HE IS OUR LIFE! He is bigger than any of those problems we may face in life. Even those problems you are facing this very moment.

I love Psalm 6:1–10, here we are given a prayer of faith in times of distress. David wrote this Psalm because he was familiar with times of stress.

> "O Lord, do not rebuke me in Your anger
> Nor chasten me in Your hot displeasure.
> Have mercy on me, O Lord, for I am weak;
> O Lord, heal me, for my bones are troubled.
> My soul also is greatly troubled;
> But You, O Lord – how long?
> Return, O Lord, deliver me!
> Oh, save me for Your mercies' sake1
> For in death there is no remembrance of You;
> In the grave who will give You thanks?
> I am weary with my groaning;

All night I make my bed swim;
I drench my couch with my tears.
My eye wastes away because of grief;
It grows old because of all my enemies.
Depart from me, all you workers of iniquity;
For the Lord has heard the voice of my weeping.
The Lord has heard my supplication;
The Lord will receive my prayer.
Let all my enemies be ashamed and greatly troubled;
Let them turn back and be ashamed suddenly."
(NSFLB)

One of the reasons God asked me to write this book was to share with you personal stories where God had me wait and rely solely on him because circumstances were out of my control. One recent storm took me back. One of those that knocks you off your feet experiences that life throws at you. I was upset, distraught, and just numb. You see my son had tried to commit suicide earlier that day. The day started out as a normal day, my son took my car to school at 8 AM because his truck was in the shop. Around 10 AM we received a phone call telling us that my son had been air lifted to another city hospital and we were to meet him there. He had tried to hang himself in the car. I had no idea what to expect. All we were told was that he was found in the vehicle with the seat belt wrapped around his neck and the seat laying all the way down into the back seat area. They broke into the vehicle and did CPR to get him breathing again, an ambulance took him to the emergency helopad where he was then flown to a Corpus Christi hospital to be treated. My husband and I got things in order at home and immediately went to the hospital where my son had been flown. Not knowing what to expect we were praying for no permanent damage. We continued to pray until we reached the hospital. While we were driving to the hospital, which was about 60 minutes away, I had texted 2 close friends and let them know what was happening, as well as my sister. They were all praying for my sons' life. As soon as we arrived at the hospital and were looking for a parking spot, my phone rang and it was the hospital telling me my son was ready to be discharged. I was speechless. I questioned whether they had the right parent. I asked them, "are you sure this is our son, the young man who was flown there from an attempted suicide? The nurse said yes ma'am. He has been checked out by the doctor and is ready to go home. I asked again if she was sure just to confirm. God performed a miracle that day. My son had no brain damage and was fine. I can tell you God still performs miracles. He saved my sons life that day. I literally had to make myself go to Bible study. There was a special Bible study that evening at a local church that I had originally planned on attending before this incident occurred. I was not really sure about attending now. I went anyway and guess what, God was there and had words of encouragement through a friend. This friend had no idea of what had happened to my son earlier that day. In fact, she was at work and God told her to take her break and go to this special bible study. He had sent her for me. She realized that and gave me the words God had given her to say, "My child, I am with you this day and I know what has taken place. I have great things for your son and have saved him for this purpose I have for him. Trust in me and follow my ways and I will direct your steps." Another confirmation that God is in control of the situation. Sometimes, it seems there is one crisis after another. God wants me to tell you to be patient because you will see how he handles things when you decide to give it to him. I can tell you that no matter how much I prayed and pleaded with God to take away this storm, to fix it, he did not. He is still working things out behind the scenes, and it is my job to simply wait and trust him to do what needs to be done.

God is steadfast in his path to do whatever needs to be done during these storms.

After I came to the conclusion that there was nothing I could do to fix this issue, I had to make the decision to "let go and let God." I know you have heard this phrase before, it was popular some years back. I had to realize and come to the place where I knew only God could work in this situation. I had to allow God to do what needed to be done in this situation. Only God knew what needed to be done. Only he can see the inside of a soul. Someone once told me, that we are continually asking God to change our circumstance and our surroundings, instead we must realize that perhaps he is working on changing us. Changing us? That's a new concept! Changing us may not be what we had in mind.

We sometimes have to literally make the decision to give the situation to him and not look back even if its someone you hold very dear. I had to give this person to God and let God do what needed to be done to make the situation better.

We have to come to the place where we realize that there is nothing we could humanly do to make it better. Nothing we can do to make a difference. Not one thing! Maybe some of you are going through a situation like this now. This is the time to give it all to God and trust him.

From that moment, we make the decision to step back, no matter what the outcome, and let God do what needs to be done in this situation. We will have complete peace and calmness about me. It is a peace that cannot really fully be described, but I know some of you have felt it at one time or another. I know this peace is from God. No matter what happens, I am going to trust God on this. We must trust God to get what needs to be done. We must trust him to change what needs to be changed. During this waiting time, we must choose to allow him to work and not interfere. Because we chose this path, we also choose to praise and worship God and thank him for all that he has done for me and my family and all that he is going to do especially in this particular situation, the peace came. God is in control. He has showed his love for me on so many levels during these times, when I decided to give him complete control. Casting Crowns has a wonderful song about praising God in the storm. It has helped me more times than I can recall when I hear it.

"I was sure by now
That You would have reached down
And wiped our tears away, stepped in and saved the day
But once again, I say, Amen and it's still raining

As the thunder rolls
I barely hear Your whisper through the rain, "I'm with you"
And as Your mercy falls I raise my hands
And praise the God who gives and takes away

And I'll praise You in this storm and I will lift my hands
For You are who You are no matter where I am
And every tear I've cried You hold in Your hand
You never left my side and though my heart is torn
I will praise You in this storm

I remember when I stumbled in the wind
You heard my cry, You raised me up again
But my strength is almost gone
How can I carry on if I can't find You

As the thunder rolls
I barely hear Your whisper through the rain, "I'm with you"
And as You mercy falls I raise my hands
And praise the God who gives and takes away

And I'll praise You in this storm and I will lift my hands
For You are who You are no matter where I am
And every tear I've cried You hold in Your hand
You never left my side and though my heart is torn
I will praise You in this storm

I lift my eyes unto the hills
Where does my help come from?
My help comes from the Lord
The Maker of Heaven and Earth

I lift my eyes unto the hills
Where does my help come from?
My help comes from the Lord
The Maker of Heaven and Earth

And I'll praise You in this storm and I will lift my hands
For You are who You are no matter where I am
And every tear I've cried You hold in Your hand
You never left my side and though my heart is torn
I will praise You in this storm
And though my heart is torn
I will praise You in this storm"

We tend to think if we have accepted Christ and we are living
a good Christian life, why would we be subjected to these trials and

storms? Why doesn't God just step in and make it better? My favorite part of this song is that we praise God during the storms. We praise God no matter what the situation is, and no matter what he answers with.

If you are facing a similar situation regarding a loved one; I urge you to give this person to God completely. *Don't look back*. God will work in that person's life as needed. Then you can move on and not worry. Worrying will not make a difference in the situation or change it in any way. It only makes you feel worse. It only allows the devil access to you. This was new territory for me, I did not know what to expect since I had never been a situation like this before and I had never given my child over to God before. Every time I felt the need to say particular things to this person, I hear God telling me to "stop," keep my mouth closed, and let him do what needs to be done. It's as if God was right there speaking to me.

I can tell you that during this time, God revealed to me great and awesome things while still working in the situation. One night, when I went to Bible study I have gone to over three years by this time, God spoke to me through a lady who also attended that same Bible study. You may ask how I knew it was God speaking through her, I knew this because the things she shared with me, she did not know, only God would have known these things and he shared them with her to tell me, so that I would believe the words were from God, himself. This lady had no idea of my circumstances, she had no idea of things that happened in the past where God revealed himself to me, yet the words that came out of her mouth were about me and the current situation and the past times, God was there with me in my life. He told me, through this lady, that I must share this experience with my group of ladies. I must let them know that God was there when we need him. He is taking care of what needs to be taken care of. With God, all things are possible. This is a fact. With him, we can get through any storm, with him, we have a more meaningful life. He loves us all so much and desires to have a personal relationship with each of us. Will you trust him today? Will you allow him to do what needs to be done? Will you allow him to carry you if necessary?

I can also tell you that things seemed to continued to get worse instead of better. No matter, each thing that happened made me put my trust in God even more. I was determined to let him be in control and step back. It is kind of like when your back goes out and you go see a Chiropractor. Sometimes, after the adjustment, your back gets worse, but with continued treatments, the back will get better. I know I also wonder why good or bad things never seem to happen to the "bad people," you know the ones who are not believing in God. Those who choose not to follow him. How come they are not being punished for their disbelief? It's almost like sometimes, bad people seem to prosper instead of just get by. If you were to look in the Bible, remember that book that gives us life's instructions, look in Jeremiah 12:1–13. Here, Jeremiah had a question for God. He also wonders why the wicked seem to prosper. (1–4) In verse 5, God answers Jeremiah specifically. This book, the Bible, truly is the answer to all of our life questions if we read it.

We also need to grow in godliness. As part of a Christian life, this is important. If we are to accomplish this, we need to learn to build a life that is characterized by a constant growing routine through all situations that we encounter. A routine is anything done on a regular basis. A sequence of actions regularly followed—a fixed program. An athlete does not get good by only practicing when they feel like it. In order to get good at something, you must practice it every day. The same is with growing in God's way. Spend time with him every day in order to be so in tune with him that we know how to proceed on the path he has designed for us. Sometimes, that time spent with him means just sitting and listening, not speaking. Sometimes, God just needs us to be still and quiet.

We need to have a growing routine to learn more about God's word. In order for us to grow, we must set aside time to be with God. We were made for this purpose. What am I saying…godliness will grow as we intentionally pursue God's wisdom and guidance. This means we purposely pursue God's wisdom. We make it a habit to seek his wisdom first. I would like to point out that this is not just for daily living, but also we need to embrace the truth of our redemption—Jesus did this for our sins. He died so we could skip all those steps of the purification in order to come into the holy place of God. Jesus is our purification. Everything is done. Jesus paid the ultimate price so we do not have to question, we never have to look back or feel unworthy. Remember, Jesus is life! Our life.

Isaiah 53:5 (NIV): "But he was pierced for our transgressions, he was crushed for our iniquities; the punishment that brought us peace was on him, and by his wounds we are healed."

Verse 3: He is despised and rejected by men, a man of sorrows and acquainted with grief, and we hid as it were our faces from him. He was despised and we did not esteem him.

Verse 4: Surely he has borne our griefs and carried our sorrows, yet we esteemed him stricken. Smitten by God and afflicted.

Loss, grief, failures, and the struggles of life do not erase the character of God. He is the same yesterday, today, and tomorrow. Hebrews 13:8 tell us, "Jesus Christ is the same yesterday, today, and forever." The struggles we face either drive us to him or propel us away from him. God is constant—he does not change. We are the ones that change.

God cares deeply for your hurts, and he is more than able to do something about them…but he does so according to his purpose… not ours. He does so according to his time; not ours.

Jesus came to rescue us from our sins, struggles, and sorrows. He came to bear all of that for us…the cross bridges that gap between God's unlimited power and his reaching love. There is no more special preparation for the select few, all are welcome.

God does care for you and he is able. When we are suffering and do not understand why, when his ways do not make sense to us, this is when we can take comfort in the rest that Jesus's love displayed on the cross is evidence of how much He loved us. He loved us this much.

In Zechariah 4:6, we discover that we do not accomplish anything by our might, it is by God's might and Spirit. "So he answered and said to me, "This is my word of the Lord to Zerubbabel: Not by might nor by power, but by My Spirit, Says the Lord of hosts."

We must stay faithful, we must keep praising God in the storms of life. If we do our part, God will do his. Each of us were put on this Earth for a specific purpose. Perhaps we do not know what that purpose is yet. Make God a priority today and see how your life will turn around. It might not happen overnight. It might take days, months, years, but one day, you will see all that God was working on. Remember, God still has the final say, no matter what your situation is, God has the last word.

In Isaiah 59:19, we discover that sometimes, living for the Lord is a real battle. The Word of God is powerful than any two-edged sword. "So shall they fear, the name of the Lord from the West, and His glory from the rising of the sun; when the enemy comes in like a flood, the Spirit of the Lord will lift up a standard against him."

I asked myself, "What is Isaiah saying exactly in this verse?" I believe this verse is telling us that God's power will come in like a flood. God will stand against Satan to protect us. What a comfort that should be.

God loves us so much. He is very aware of the bad medical report, the lost job, the low finances. God can restore your marriage. He knows of that addiction your son or daughter has. He already knows the situation even before we send up prayers to Him regarding it. "God's light will come in on your darkness. (John 1:5, "And the light shines in the darkness, and the darkness did not comprehend it.") Keep praising him, keep believing that he can do what he says he can do. Keep believing that he is big enough! It is a choice to build your faith up and trust.

I believe that sometimes God uses obstacles in our lives to push us, to expand our territory, (so to speak). He sometimes needs to refine us and this is how He goes about that process. Some call it pruning. You can find many references to this process, I like Psalm 12:6, " The words of the Lord are pure words, Like silver tried in a furnace of earth, purified seven times." 1 Peter 1:7, "That the genuineness of your faith, being much more precious than gold that perishes, though it is tested by fire, may be found to praise, honor, and glory at the revelation of Jesus Christ." Psalm 66:10, "For You, O God have tested us; you have refined us as silver is refined." This process is not always pleasant, but sometimes required in order that we become the person God has planned us to be. God can use obstacles in your life to promote you. He chooses this way so that you can tell others about his great and mighty works in your life (Psalm 92:5). There are many more verses in the Bible which refer to God's mighty works.

I hope this book encourages those having a tough time, those going through some hard trials and struggles. If God were not in my life, I would not be able to handle these trials. At my utmost lowest point, God speaks to me either through a song on the Christian radio station or through people He has placed in my life. He always knows what I need and when I need it. That is the kind of God we serve! He is always there to lift us up, even when we feel alone. We are not alone. God is with us 24/7. Sometimes you have to be open and listen to God in order to hear or see what he is doing as encouragement for you at the time.

Heavenly Father, we thank you for guiding our lives as your will directs and for showing us your mercy each and every day. We thank you for performing miracles still today and for showing us unending love no matter what we have done and will do. We ask today that you give us continued wisdom and guidance for the path you have chosen for each of us.

In Jesus' name I pray these things
Amen

MORE THAN ENOUGH

And God is able to make all grace abound to you,
So that having all sufficiency in all things,
At all times, you may abound in every good work.
2 Corinthians 9:8

I want this book to be an encouragement for others so that they can look for the good during the difficult times of life. With God, all things are possible. This is a fact. We must not limit God because of our human capacities. What seems impossible to us is never impossible to God.

In 2 Kings, there is a story of a widow, she is broke and her sons are going to be taken away from her in exchange for her past due bills. All she has of any value is a small pot of oil. Elisha stops by to see her. He instructs her to go to the neighbors, and get all the empty pots they have. Get all the pots she can carry and bring them back to her house. She thinks the instruction seems odd, but does what he asks. He then instructs her to pour the oil she has into one of those empty pots. When she does this, the oil just keeps pouring, filling up all the empty pots she brought back.

This woman new the reality she could see. I have this much oil and that is it. How will this little oil fill up all these pots you have instructed me to gather?

2 Kings 4:1–7
A certain woman of the wives of the sons
of the prophets cried out to Elisha, saying,
"Your servant my husband is dead,
and you know that your servant feared the Lord.
And the creditor is coming
to take my two sons to be his slaves."
So Elisha said to her, "What shall I do for you?
Tell me, what do you have in the house?"
and she said, "Your maidservant has nothing
in the house but a jar of oil." Then he said,
"Go borrow vessels from everywhere;
do not gather just a few. And when you have come in,
you shall shut the door behind you and your sons;
then pour it into all those vessels,
and set aside the full ones."
So she went from him and shut the door
behind her and her sons, who brought the vessels to her;
and she poured it out. Now it came to pass,
when the vessels were full, that she said to her son,
"Bring me another vessel." And he said to her,
"There is not another vessel." So the oil ceased.
Then she came and told the man of God.
And he said, "Go, sell the oil and pay your debt;
] and you and your sons live on the rest."

This woman trusted God through Elisha. Because of her trust, God's infinite power took over and the oil kept coming. Even though things didn't make sense. Even though in the reality, it seemed impossible. With God, all things are possible.

Our God is powerful, he can supernaturally multiple anything in our lives. We must not limit his power by our small thinking. Our God is the "El Shaddai." This means he is the god of more than enough. Don't waste your time trying to figure out how God is going to do something. Just put it in his hands and let him do what he needs to do. Think about it, if he created the entire earth and all the things in it over six days, then why would he not be able to handle your issues? He is big enough.

It is never our job to try and figure out how God will do something. It is also never our job to try and help God do something. I think sometimes, when we try to help, we end up making matters worse. We prolong the trials because with our so-called help, we have made God have to work longer and harder to fix the problem.

God's ways are not our ways. That is why we cannot possible imagine the solution to problems. We are thinking like man and not like God. It is not our place to think like God, don't misunderstand me. It is not our job to figure out how things will be fixed. It is our job to trust. It is our job to have faith and believe God is big enough.

In 2 Peter 3:8, we see that God's days are not like our days. "But, Beloved, do not forget this one thing, that with the Lord one day is a thousand years, and a thousand years as one day." 1000=1. Psalm 90:4 states this very same thing. If we look at it numerically, it does not make any sense; God's time and our time are not the same and that is something we should just believe and accept.

Romans 4:13–25 talks about Abraham and his great faith of believing God when he told Abraham and Sarah they would have a child.

Verses 17–20, 17 "(as it is written, "I have made you a father of many nations" in the presence of Him who he believed—God, who gives life to the dead and calls those things which do not exist as though they did;

18 who, contrary to hope, in hope believed, so that he became the father of many nations, according to what was spoken, So shall your descendants be."

19 And not being weak in faith, he did not consider his own body, already dead (since he was about 100 years old) and the deadness of Sarah's womb.

20 He did not waiver at the promise of God through unbelief, but was strengthened in faith, giving glory to God." This prophecy seemed impossible.

Whatever you are going through right now, if you have prayed and asked God to work in this situation, he will. Verse 20 tells us that Abraham, in spite of being so old, did not disbelieve God when he was told that he and his wife would have a child. "He did not waiver at the promise of God through unbelief, but was strengthened in faith, giving glory to God."

We become stronger when we trust God to take control of the very thing we are praying about. Just like Abraham, we can become strengthened in our faith because we chose to give God all the glory and praise before we see the answer. Abraham chose to believe no matter how the present circumstances appeared. No matter that he was 100 years old, and Sarah was in her nineties. In fact, Abraham had to wait twenty-five years for God to fulfill that promise made to him. He trusted God to do what he said he would do. Trust is a difficult thing to do when those around us have let us down.

One of the reasons I had to move back to my small home town after being gone for over 15 years was because my husband had made some bad choices and was going to go to Federal Prison for 24 months. This move was going to be hard on all of us. My children had to adjust to a new town, new schools, new people and then worst of all, lose their father for 24 months. In fact during the first 6 months after my husband went to prison, my 14 year old son was in a dirt bike accident and broke both his legs, our family dog was diagnosed with cancer and we had to put him to sleep, and finally my brother passed away. Talk about overload. I was on it. All of these things happened while my husband was gone, I had to deal with them on my own. It was not easy. I tried to think of the positive instead of the negative and this helped tremendously. When I look back at those days I see so much of how God was there during all those situations. He was with us every step of the way.

Sometimes, the outcome of a situation is more detailed than we realize. We do not see what is happening behind the scenes. We only see what is on the outside. We do not see what is messed up and needs to be fixed from the inside. At this point, this is when we need to trust God more!

Things take place in God's time and never our time. This seems to be a problem with us as Christians/humans. We cannot seem to understand the time difference. Since we live in a "microwave" world, we expect to see results quickly. This is not how God usually works. Don't get me wrong, he still performs miracles every day. Some things just take longer because he is working on the inside.

As I mentioned before, if we used the time we had while we wait on God to praise and worship him, we would be less likely to keep worrying about the situation?

Perhaps we need to change our thinking out praise and worship. We tend to only praise and worship God when we have the situation resolved, instead of praise and worship while we are waiting for the answer. It is just as important to praise and worship him while we wait as it is when he answers. In Philippians 4:4–7, we are told, "Rejoice in the Lord always. Again I will say, rejoice! Let your gentleness be known to all men. The Lord is at hand. Be anxious for nothing, but in everything by prayer and supplication, with thanksgiving, let your requests be made known to God; and the peace of God, which surpasses all understanding, will guard your hearts and minds through Christ Jesus."

1 Thessalonians 5:16 tells us to "Rejoice always."

What if instead of continuing to ask God over and over again about a situation that we cannot see any change in, what if we asked once and then praised and worshiped God until the situation was resolved? Just like the song states, I will praise you in this storm. There is another song called, Eye of the Storm, by Ryan Stevenson. The lyrics state that in the eye of the storm or in the midst of trials and problems, God remains in control and in the middle of the war, God is guarding our soul. God is our anchor through the storms of life. No matter what the circumstance, God remains in control.

So think about it. We would be thanking God in advance for the answer. No matter what it turns out to be. We would be trusting him to answer us and praising him for it ahead of time. Unheard of?

What if we tried it just to see. I can assure you that when you are praising God, your trials seem smaller. This is how we strengthen our faith. The burden will become lighter because you are putting all those negative thoughts and doubts into a positive atmosphere. You are releasing God to do what he needs to do in the situation.

Once you have sent up prayers for that situation, leave it be. Let God do what he needs to do. The more we dwell on the issue, the more we start to doubt and question. This decreases our faith. This also gives the devil an opportunity to send out negative thoughts to enhance our fear and frustration.

2 Peter 3:14–17 talks about being steadfast, 14"Therefore, beloved, looking forward to these things, be diligent to be found by Him in peace, without spot and blameless;

15 and consider that the longsuffering of our Lord is salvation—as also our beloved brother Paul, according to the wisdom given to him, has written to you,

16 as also in all his "epistles, speaking in them of these things, in which are some things hard to understand, which untaught and unstable people twist to their own destruction, as they do also the rest of the Scriptures.

17 You therefore, beloved, since you know this beforehand, beware lest you also fall from your own steadfastness being led away with the error of the wicked; but grow in the grace and knowledge of our Lord and Savior Jesus Christ."

Lets step off the rollercoaster and learn to trust God in all our situations. God has promised us that he will be with us during the storms, so trust him to do so now.

Heavenly Father,

We thank you for all the trials in our lives because we know that these trials make us stronger and help us to become the person who created us to be. We do realize that you are more than enough for us, Lord. Give us your continued guidance and wisdom each day so that we may become more like you.

In Jesus name I pray these things
Amen

BELIEVE IT OR NOT

But let him ask in faith, with no doubting,
For he who doubts is like a wave
Of the sea driven and tossed by the wind.
James 1:6

James 1:6–8 tells us to believe when we ask for something. "But when you ask, you must believe and not doubt, because the one who doubts is like a wave of the sea, blown and tossed by the wind. That person should not expect to receive anything from the Lord. Such a person is double-minded and unstable in all they do."

If we become sick and start making our own funeral plans and at the same time we are believing God to heal us, we are not focusing on our God; we are focusing on our problem. God always keeps his word and he never breaks any promises. Just because you have not heard from him immediately, does not mean he is not working behind the scenes. Sometimes, there are more things to work out than you even realize. Remember, sometimes there is a bigger mess to work on that you cannot see. God has a way of getting your needs met. It is called seed faith. Our faith in God should be like a seed. If we will put our faith into action (when we release it to God), the issue will take on a new perspective.

Perhaps you are waiting during this trial because God is trying to build up your character. Perhaps he is trying to teach you patience. All things are for God's glory and not ours. It is not about us! We may never know the purpose, and that is okay. If God didn't have a reason, he would not have put it in our pathway. First, you must have faith, then faith becomes active by hearing the word of God, then you act on that faith. When something does not turn out like you thought it was going to, we get discouraged and feel abandoned by God. The truth is and we should believe that God has something better in store for us and we should look forward to what he is planning.

Did you ever think that perhaps God is not answering your prayer yet because you are not ready to receive it? Perhaps God sees that you need some changes or that person you are praying about needs some changes before things move into place. No matter what is going on, God's timing will be perfect. You can bet your life on it. Will you praise him during this time anyway. Will you thank him in advance for the things He will do in that particular situation. Praise God for the good that only he can provide from your trials. During the time when I first moved back to my hometown and all those trials hit me and my children over that 6 month period, when I look back I see a positive. I realized God was letting me spend more time with my brother, who passed away about one year after I moved back to my home town. During that year prior to his death, my brother moved about 3 hours away and he still had work and doctors in my area. So every 3-4 weeks for one whole year he would come down and stay with me and the children, anywhere from 2-3 days while he did what he needed to do. It was the most I had seen of my older brother in my entire life. Well I guess God knew the outcome, so I believe he allowed me to spend those precious moments with my brother during that last year of his life. In fact, the weekend that my brother passed away, the children and I were at his house visiting with him. My daughter was going to tour Baylor University and see if she wanted to go to school there, and so we decided to spend the weekend with my brother. I left my 2 boys who were 13 and 10 with my brother and his wife for the day while my daughter and I drove to Waco and took a look at Baylor. It was a last minute trip to stay with my brother as we were originally going to stay in a motel since my directions had told me it was out of the way to go to where my brother lived. My brother called me several times and finally explained a direct route from his house to the university so it was not that far after all and we would get to stay at his house and visit for the labor day weekend. This was totally a God thing!

God was also allowing my children to become closer with their paternal grandparents since they also lived in the small town as us. They were with the children and I during all of those difficult struggles and helped us so much with their love and support.

Did you know that when you continually give God praise no matter what the circumstances are, you will see that your strength is mightier than you thought. You become strong and faith filled. You will also experience a peace that cannot be explained. This peace can only come from God. He does not want us to worry and be anxious for anything. He wants to handle our trials and give us the peace we need to be still. Let's start changing our perspective about praying and see how much better we handle things.

There is a story in the Bible about Daniel. He prayed to God for a particular situation and it took twenty-one days for the angel to arrive after he prayed. Daniel was upset that it took so long for his prayer to be answered, "Then he said to me, do not fear, Daniel, for from the first day that you set your heart to understand, and to humble yourself before your God, your words were heard, and I have come because of your words. But the prince of the kingdom of Persia withstood me for 21 days." So you see, as soon as Daniel prayed, God dispatched the angel to go and help him, but the angel was not able to get there right away because he was fighting those principalities that we do not see. All those spirit warfare, things are happening around us all the time. God sees behind the scenes where we cannot, so let him work.

John 11:14–40 has some insight on this. Verse 40, "Did I not tell you that if you believe, you will see the Glory of God." Sometimes, we do not get the answer right away because God has an awesome plan where his glory will be revealed.

Another example is in 1 Kings, here Elijah prays for God to take away the rain and send in a drought. Then he prays for God to send rain. 1 Kings 18:41–45, "Then Elijah said to Ahab, "Go up, eat and drink; for there is the sound of abundance of rain." So Ahab went up to eat and drink. And Elijah went up to the top of Carmel; then he bowed down on the ground, and put his face between his knees, and said to his servant, "Go up now, look toward the sea. So the servant went and looked up aid, there is nothing." And seven times, he did this and seven times, he came back and saw no clouds or rain. Instead of giving up, Elisha trusted God, even for the rain. Elijah told him to go once more, this time he saw a cloud as it began to rain. Wait upon the Lord, for he will answer you.

Elijah trusted God and believed that God would bring the rain and that is why he kept sending his servant to go look. This is an awesome demonstration of how God revealed his glory.

Depending on what you are going through, you may not feel like praising God, but friend I am asking you to do it anyway.

Did you know that praising God does three things:

Builds and strengthens our faith
Takes focus away from the problem
Gives God all the Glory

We should be thanking God for desiring communication with us, his people. For your reassurance that he is indeed listening and ready to help in our time of need. Help us to learn that you do hear us the first time. Give us the peace that surpasses all understanding so that we can learn to praise you in the storms instead of begging and pleading, and worrying about the situation. Help us to develop the habit of constantly sending you praises no matter what we are going through. We know you never give us more than we can handle and we just want to thank you for all you do and will continue to do on our behalf.

I remember a time when my daughter had just left the house headed for a early bus ride to a school tennis tournament. It was around 5 Am when she left the house, not even 5 minutes passed when I received a phone call from her phone, but not her voice, telling me she had been in a horrible car accident and that I needed to come. I quickly got dressed and headed about 2 miles down the road from my house where the accident had occurred. The vehicle she had been driving was completely totaled and laying upside down in a pasture. My daughter was laying down on the side of the road in the grass, covered with a jacket and the people who had stopped to help her had given her some water. They preceded to tell me that she seemed ok, but that they had called the ambulance and it should be arriving shortly. They stayed with us until the ambulance arrived.

I looked around and saw the vehicle upside down, all the windows had been broken and the roof was crushed in on the driver side. I asked her how she could have possibly gotten out of the vehicle since the doors were also smashed in. She said she craweled out of the back area and through the back side broken window. She told me that the car started spinning around, probably from a blown out tire, she then hit the gate going sideways and flipped over the burm, (this burm was placed there to protect a gas pipeline) where she continued to flip about 5 more times before landing on the roof of the car. From what I could see, she only had small cuts all over from the broken glass. She had one larger cut on top of her head where the roof has crushed down on top of her. Thank goodness she had been wearing her seat belt. They kept her from being thrown from the vehicle. Also the vehicle she had been driving was an older model and had been made of heavy metal versus the lighter metal they use on all cars today. The ambulance finally arrived and she was headed to the ER. I had to wait behind for the DPS and also the wrecker service to pick up the vehicle. The wrecker service arrived on the scene next. The man asked me how the driver was, I said she appeared to be fine. He preceded to tell me that from the condition of the vehicle, he didn't think the driver had survived. WOW! I also suspected the same. I knew God had his angels working overtime on that accident. You see, one never knows when things like this will take place. Yet, thank goodness God is in control and can handle the situation even when we are not aware of what is going on. He allowed her car to flip over the burm, which in this case gave the car height enough to not hit the gas pipeline.

I want to stress again that our God is bigger than any obstacle you are facing now or will face in the future. This is where faith comes in. Just because you cannot see a way does not mean that there is not one. Don't limit God's power just because you cannot see it.

Our God can and will do impossible things for his children. God will always arm you with strength for the battle you are facing. (Psalm 18:39, "For you have armed me with strength for the battle; You have subdued under me those who rose up against me.") He will also allow you to see the truth in your situation. (Psalm 119:18, "Open my eyes so that I may see wondrous things from your law.") God will revive you while you go through these trials. Psalm 138:7, "Though I walk in the midst of trouble, you will revive me; You will stretch out your hand against the wrath of my enemies, and your right hand will save me."

God's power supersedes human power, that includes the laws of medicine, laws of science, laws of physics, laws of banking, and any other human laws you can think of. Don't consider your circumstance, consider your God. He is the "Great I Am." He is everything you will ever need. He is the healer, the provider, the peace, the friend, the deliverer. God's power supersedes.

Our God can stop the sun for Joshua (Joshua 10:12–13,
"Then Joshua spoke to the Lord in the day when the
Lord delivered up the Amorites before the children
of Israel, and he said in the sight of Israel:
'Sun, stand still over Gibeon;
And Moon, in the Valley of Aijalon.'
So the sun stood still,
And the noon stopped,
Till the people had revenge
Upon their enemies.

Is this not written in the Book of Jasher? So the sun stood still in the midst of heaven, and did not hasten to go down for about a whole day."

Our God can protect Daniel from the lions (Daniel 6:16–22),
16 "So the king gave the command, and they brought Daniel and
cast *him* into the den of lions. *But* the king spoke, saying to Daniel,
"Your God, whom you serve continually, He will deliver you."

17 Then a stone was brought and laid on the mouth of the den,
and the king sealed it with his own signet ring and with the signets of
his lords, that the purpose concerning Daniel might not be changed."

18 Now the king went to this palace and spent the night fasting;
and no musicians were brought before him. Also his sleep went from
him.

19 Then the king arose very early in the morning and went in
haste to the den of lions.

20 And when he came to the den, he cried out with a lamenting
voice to Daniel. The king spoke, saying to Daniel, "Daniel, servant
of the living God, has your God, whom you serve continually, been
able to deliver you from the lions?

21 Then Daniel said to the king, "O king, live forever."

22 My God sent His angels and shut the lions mouths, so that
they have not hurt me, because I was found innocent before Him;
and also, O king, I have done no wrong before you."

Our God can feed five thousand people with loaves of bread
(Matthew 14:13–21,

13 "When Jesus heard *it*, He departed from there by boat to a
deserted place by Himself. But when the multitudes heard it, they
followed Him on foot from the cities.

14 And when Jesus went out He saw a great multitude; and He
was moved with compassion for them, and healed their sick.

15 When it was evening, His disciples came to Him saying, This
is a deserted place, and the hour is already late. Send the multitudes
away, that they may go into the villages and buy themselves food.

16 But Jesus said to them, "They do not need to go away. You give them something to eat."

17 And they said to Him, We have here only five loaves and two fish.

18 He said, "Bring them here to Me."

19 Then He commanded the multitudes to sit down on the grass. And he took the five loaves and the two fish, and looking up to heaven, He blessed and broke and gave the loaves to the disciples; and the disciples gave to the multitudes.

20 So they all ate and were filled and they took up twelve baskets full of the fragments that remained.

21 Now those who had eaten were about five thousand men, besides women and children."

Mark 6:30–42, 30"Then the apostles gathered to Jesus and told Him all things, both what they had done and what they had taught.

31 And He said to them, "Come aside by yourselves to a deserted place and rest a while." For there were many coming and going, and they did not even have time to eat.

32 So they departed to a deserted place in the boat by themselves.

33 But the multitudes saw them departing, and many knew Him and ran there on foot from all the cities. They arrived before them and came together to Him.

34 And Jesus, when He came out, saw a great multitude and was moved with compassion for them, because they were like sheep not having a shepherd. So He began to teach them many things.

35 When the day was now far spent, His disciples came to Him and said, This is a deserted place, and already thee hour is late.

36 Send them away, that they may go into the surrounding country, and villages and buy themselves bread for they have nothing to eat.

37 But He answered them and said to them, "You give them something to eat." And they said to Him, "Shall we go and buy two hundred denarii worth of bread and give them something to eat?"

38 But He said to them, "How many loaves do you have? Go and see." And when they found out they said, "Five loaves and two fish."

39 Then He commanded them to make them all sit down in groups on the green grass.

40 So they sat down in ranks, in hundreds and in fifties.

41 And when He had taken the five loaves and the two fish, He looked up to heaven blessed and broke the loaves and gave them to his disciples to set before them; and the two fish He divided among them all. So they all ate and were filled.

Our God can turn water into wine. (John 2:1–10, 1 "On the third day there was a wedding in Cana of Galilee, and the mother of Jesus was there.

2 Now both Jesus and His disciples were invited to the wedding.

3 And when they ran out of wine, the mother of Jesus said to Him, "They have no wine."

4 Jesus said to her, "Woman, what does your concern have to do with me? My hour has not yet come."

5 His mother said to the servants, Whatever He says to you, do it.

6 Now there were set there six water pots of stone, according to the manner of purification of the Jews, containing twenty or thirty gallons apiece.

7 Jesus said to them, "Fill the water pots with water." and they filled them up to the brim.

8 And He said to them, "Draw some out now, and take it to the master of the feast." And they took it.

9 When the aster of the feast had tasted the water that was made wine, and did not know where it came from (but the servants who had drawn the water knew), the master of the feast called the bridegroom.

10 And he said to him, "Every man at the beginning sets out the good wine, and when the guests have well drunk, then the inferior. You have kept the good wine until now!"

Our God can change your circumstances now! Trust him to do the impossible. Impossible can be defined as "not able to occur, exist, or be done." Is your situation impossible today? God can do the impossible. The power of promise of God's word involves a balanced perspective. Abraham's story is an excellent example because he believed God even though the circumstances were not the best. God calls those things which do not exist as though they do exist. Romans 4:20, "He did not waver at the promise of God through unbelief, but was strengthened in faith, giving glory to God."

We must start changing our focus and allow God's power to come to the rescue. He can do it. He is big enough. Did you know that it takes the same amount of energy to worry about something as it does to believe God about that something?

Today is the day! Thank God for his all powerful might and his everlasting love for you. Thank him for being in control and giving you guidance, patience, and peace during the storm.

Be strong in the Lord as Ephesians 6:10 tells us, "When God becomes bigger, our problems will seem smaller." We must not dwell on the problems. Praise God for what he is going to do.

He is going to do mighty works. Our God is faithful.

Sometimes, our knowledge of things prevents us from allowing God to work. We simply know too much for our own good. We try to reason with the problem. The numbers don't add up, so there is no way I can pay all my bills this month. The doctor said I have cancer, he is smart and knows all. I guess I will die.

We need to learn to turn off our minds and all the negative thoughts. We must remember that it does not matter what we have been told or what we hear from friends or family members, God's ways are not our ways. His days are not the same, his time is not our time.

With God, the impossible can happen and it does not have to make sense. It does not have to add up. God is the all powerful creator of the universe. Trust him to make a way when there is no way. Push back all those negative thoughts and allow him to work.

Proverbs 3:5–6 tells us,
"Trust in the Lord with all your heart,
And lean no ton your own understanding;
In all your ways submit to Him,
And he will make your paths straight."

When our plans do not work out and seem quite different than what we imagined. When dreams become delayed or interrupted, don't give up! This is when you need to dig in, Folks! Just because you have a slow down or set back is not telling us, we did something wrong, it's not telling us we will never accomplish this dream. Remember, God always works from an entire perspective of things from the inside out. Sometimes, there are things deep down in our or someone else that needs to be worked on, worked out before the entire situation gets clear.

If you had an open wound that was infected, you would not want the doctor to just close it up without cleaning it out first, would you? No, you would want the doctor to clean it out and then sew it up. This is exactly how God works also.

Luke 5:37, "And no one pours new wine into old wineskins. Otherwise, the new wine will burst the skins, the wine will run out and the wineskins will be ruined." Sometimes, in order for us to realize the dreams God put in us, we have to move make changes from within. We have to let go of the old, leave those things behind you. We have to get ready for the new God has in store.

Remember James 1:6–8 tells us to believe when we ask. God does keep his word and will be there to do what is necessary.

Heavenly Father,

Thank you for allowing obstacles to come our way to build up our strength and our faith in you. Thank you for taking the focus away from our problems and showing us blessings in disguise during these difficult times.

We thank you also for giving us what we ask for, if it is in your will to do so. We give you all the glory this day and every day.

In Jesus' name we pray these things
Amen

ABOUT THE AUTHOR

Robbin Stone Stasny grew up in a small town, after getting married, she moved away for many years but eventually came back to the small town because of difficult circumstances. She was taught Christian values as a young girl by her mother, who passed away when Robbin was twenty. This death was the first difficult experience Robbin had ever encountered and pushed her toward a stronger relationship with God in learning how to deal with life's tough times. From that point on, she learned to lean on the Lord for all things because he was her strength during life's difficult times. During the next eight years of her life, after moving back to the small town, Philippians 4:13 became her families basic scripture in dealing with the numerous trials that came their way. Changing their focus to God during life's difficult situations helped each of them become strong in the Lord. When our God becomes bigger, life's problems become smaller.